Restaura

A
TO
Z Adventure

A KELLY GREER PUBLICATION
ISBN: 979-8991109871

"Food brings people together on many different levels. It's nourishment of the soul and body; it's truly love."
– Giada De Laurentiis

Date: _____

Where to Dine?
List a few spots you're considering for this letter-choices make it fun!:

The Winner Is...
Write your pick and note what made it stand out:

Savor the Moment!
Share a quick highlight of your experience-the dishes, vibe, and details:

Rating: ☆☆☆☆☆

Memory Lane...
Snap a photo that captures the moment, be sure to get the name in the shot, so you'll always remember this stop of your journey!

Who Shared This Meal?
Whether you were solo, with friends, or family, describe who joined you!

Date: _____

Where to Dine?
List a few spots you're considering for this letter-choices make it fun!:

The Winner Is...
Write your pick and note what made it stand out:

Savor the Moment!
Share a quick highlight of your experience-the dishes, vibe, and details:

Rating: ☆☆☆☆☆

Memory Lane...
 Snap a photo that captures the moment, be sure to get the name in the shot, so you'll always remember this stop of your journey!

Who Shared This Meal?
 Whether you were solo, with friends, or family, describe who joined you!

Date: _____

Where to Dine?
List a few spots you're considering for this letter-choices make it fun!:

The Winner Is...
Write your pick and note what made it stand out:

Savor the Moment!
Share a quick highlight of your experience-the dishes, vibe, and details:

Rating: ☆☆☆☆☆

Memory Lane...
Snap a photo that captures the moment, be sure to get the name in the shot, so you'll always remember this stop of your journey!

Who Shared This Meal?
Whether you were solo, with friends, or family, describe who joined you!

Date: _____

D

Where to Dine?
List a few spots you're considering for this letter-choices make it fun!:

The Winner Is...
Write your pick and note what made it stand out:

Savor the Moment!
Share a quick highlight of your experience-the dishes, vibe, and details:

Rating: ☆☆☆☆☆

Memory Lane...
Snap a photo that captures the moment, be sure to get the name in the shot, so you'll always remember this stop of your journey!

Who Shared This Meal?
Whether you were solo, with friends, or family, describe who joined you!

Date: _____

Where to Dine?
List a few spots you're considering for this letter-choices make it fun!:

The Winner Is...
Write your pick and note what made it stand out:

Savor the Moment!
Share a quick highlight of your experience-the dishes, vibe, and details:

Rating: ☆☆☆☆☆

Memory Lane...
Snap a photo that captures the moment, be sure to get the name in the shot, so you'll always remember this stop of your journey!

Who Shared This Meal?
Whether you were solo, with friends, or family, describe who joined you!

Date: _____

Where to Dine?
List a few spots you're considering for this letter-choices make it fun!:

The Winner Is...
Write your pick and note what made it stand out:

Savor the Moment!
Share a quick highlight of your experience-the dishes, vibe, and details:

Rating: ☆☆☆☆☆

Memory Lane...
Snap a photo that captures the moment, be sure to get the name in the shot, so you'll always remember this stop of your journey!

Who Shared This Meal?
Whether you were solo, with friends, or family, describe who joined you!

Date: _____

G

Where to Dine?
List a few spots you're considering for this letter-choices make it fun!:

The Winner Is...
Write your pick and note what made it stand out:

Savor the Moment!
Share a quick highlight of your experience-the dishes, vibe, and details:

Rating: ☆☆☆☆☆

Memory Lane...
Snap a photo that captures the moment, be sure to get the name in the shot, so you'll always remember this stop of your journey!

Who Shared This Meal?
Whether you were solo, with friends, or family, describe who joined you!

Date: _____

H

Where to Dine?
List a few spots you're considering for this letter-choices make it fun!:

The Winner Is...
Write your pick and note what made it stand out:

Savor the Moment!
Share a quick highlight of your experience-the dishes, vibe, and details:

Rating: ☆☆☆☆☆

Memory Lane...
Snap a photo that captures the moment, be sure to get the name in the shot, so you'll always remember this stop of your journey!

Who Shared This Meal?
Whether you were solo, with friends, or family, describe who joined you!

Date: _____

I

Where to Dine?
List a few spots you're considering for this letter-choices make it fun!:

The Winner Is...
Write your pick and note what made it stand out:

Savor the Moment!
Share a quick highlight of your experience-the dishes, vibe, and details:

Rating: ☆☆☆☆☆

Memory Lane...
Snap a photo that captures the moment, be sure to get the name in the shot, so you'll always remember this stop of your journey!

Who Shared This Meal?
Whether you were solo, with friends, or family, describe who joined you!

Date: _____

J

Where to Dine?
List a few spots you're considering for this letter-choices make it fun!:

The Winner Is...
Write your pick and note what made it stand out:

Savor the Moment!
Share a quick highlight of your experience-the dishes, vibe, and details:

Rating: ☆☆☆☆☆

Memory Lane...
Snap a photo that captures the moment, be sure to get the name in the shot, so you'll always remember this stop of your journey!

Who Shared This Meal?
Whether you were solo, with friends, or family, describe who joined you!

Date: _____

Where to Dine?
List a few spots you're considering for this letter-choices make it fun!:

The Winner Is...
Write your pick and note what made it stand out:

Savor the Moment!
Share a quick highlight of your experience-the dishes, vibe, and details:

Rating: ☆☆☆☆☆

Memory Lane...
Snap a photo that captures the moment, be sure to get the name in the shot, so you'll always remember this stop of your journey!

Who Shared This Meal?
Whether you were solo, with friends, or family, describe who joined you!

Date: _____

Where to Dine?
List a few spots you're considering for this letter-choices make it fun!:

The Winner Is...
Write your pick and note what made it stand out:

Savor the Moment!
Share a quick highlight of your experience-the dishes, vibe, and details:

Rating: ☆☆☆☆☆

Memory Lane...

Snap a photo that captures the moment, be sure to get the name in the shot, so you'll always remember this stop of your journey!

Who Shared This Meal?

Whether you were solo, with friends, or family, describe who joined you!

Date: _____

Where to Dine?
List a few spots you're considering for this letter-choices make it fun!:

The Winner Is...
Write your pick and note what made it stand out:

Savor the Moment!
Share a quick highlight of your experience-the dishes, vibe, and details:

Rating: ☆☆☆☆☆

Memory Lane...
Snap a photo that captures the moment, be sure to get the name in the shot, so you'll always remember this stop of your journey!

Who Shared This Meal?
Whether you were solo, with friends, or family, describe who joined you!

Date: _____

Where to Dine?
List a few spots you're considering for this letter-choices make it fun!:

The Winner Is...
Write your pick and note what made it stand out:

Savor the Moment!
Share a quick highlight of your experience-the dishes, vibe, and details:

Rating: ☆☆☆☆☆

Memory Lane...
Snap a photo that captures the moment, be sure to get the name in the shot, so you'll always remember this stop of your journey!

Who Shared This Meal?
Whether you were solo, with friends, or family, describe who joined you!

Date: _____

Where to Dine?
List a few spots you're considering for this letter-choices make it fun!:

The Winner Is...
Write your pick and note what made it stand out:

Savor the Moment!
Share a quick highlight of your experience-the dishes, vibe, and details:

Rating: ☆☆☆☆☆

Memory Lane...
Snap a photo that captures the moment, be sure to get the name in the shot, so you'll always remember this stop of your journey!

Who Shared This Meal?
Whether you were solo, with friends, or family, describe who joined you!

Date: _____

Where to Dine?
List a few spots you're considering for this letter-choices make it fun!:

The Winner Is...
Write your pick and note what made it stand out:

Savor the Moment!
Share a quick highlight of your experience-the dishes, vibe, and details:

Rating: ☆☆☆☆☆

Memory Lane...
Snap a photo that captures the moment, be sure to get the name in the shot, so you'll always remember this stop of your journey!

Who Shared This Meal?
Whether you were solo, with friends, or family, describe who joined you!

Date: _____

Where to Dine?
List a few spots you're considering for this letter-choices make it fun!:

The Winner Is...
Write your pick and note what made it stand out:

Savor the Moment!
Share a quick highlight of your experience-the dishes, vibe, and details:

Rating: ☆☆☆☆☆

Memory Lane...
Snap a photo that captures the moment, be sure to get the name in the shot, so you'll always remember this stop of your journey!

Who Shared This Meal?
Whether you were solo, with friends, or family, describe who joined you!

Date: _____

Where to Dine?
List a few spots you're considering for this letter-choices make it fun!:

The Winner Is...
Write your pick and note what made it stand out:

Savor the Moment!
Share a quick highlight of your experience-the dishes, vibe, and details:

Rating: ☆☆☆☆☆

Memory Lane...
Snap a photo that captures the moment, be sure to get the name in the shot, so you'll always remember this stop of your journey!

Who Shared This Meal?
Whether you were solo, with friends, or family, describe who joined you!

Date: _____

Where to Dine?
List a few spots you're considering for this letter-choices make it fun!:

The Winner Is...
Write your pick and note what made it stand out:

Savor the Moment!
Share a quick highlight of your experience-the dishes, vibe, and details:

Rating: ☆☆☆☆☆

Memory Lane...
Snap a photo that captures the moment, be sure to get the name in the shot, so you'll always remember this stop of your journey!

Who Shared This Meal?
Whether you were solo, with friends, or family, describe who joined you!

Date: _____   *T*

Where to Dine?
List a few spots you're considering for this letter-choices make it fun!:

The Winner Is...
Write your pick and note what made it stand out:

Savor the Moment!
Share a quick highlight of your experience-the dishes, vibe, and details:

Rating: ☆☆☆☆☆

Memory Lane...
Snap a photo that captures the moment, be sure to get the name in the shot, so you'll always remember this stop of your journey!

Who Shared This Meal?
Whether you were solo, with friends, or family, describe who joined you!

Date: _____

Where to Dine?
List a few spots you're considering for this letter-choices make it fun!:

The Winner Is...
Write your pick and note what made it stand out:

Savor the Moment!
Share a quick highlight of your experience-the dishes, vibe, and details:

Rating: ☆☆☆☆☆

Memory Lane...
Snap a photo that captures the moment, be sure to get the name in the shot, so you'll always remember this stop of your journey!

Who Shared This Meal?
Whether you were solo, with friends, or family, describe who joined you!

Date: _____

Where to Dine?
List a few spots you're considering for this letter-choices make it fun!:

The Winner Is...
Write your pick and note what made it stand out:

Savor the Moment!
Share a quick highlight of your experience-the dishes, vibe, and details:

Rating: ☆☆☆☆☆

Memory Lane...
 Snap a photo that captures the moment, be sure to get the name in the shot, so you'll always remember this stop of your journey!

Who Shared This Meal?
 Whether you were solo, with friends, or family, describe who joined you!

Date: _____

Where to Dine?
List a few spots you're considering for this letter-choices make it fun!:

The Winner Is...
Write your pick and note what made it stand out:

Savor the Moment!
Share a quick highlight of your experience-the dishes, vibe, and details:

Rating: ☆☆☆☆☆

Memory Lane...
Snap a photo that captures the moment, be sure to get the name in the shot, so you'll always remember this stop of your journey!

Who Shared This Meal?
Whether you were solo, with friends, or family, describe who joined you!

Date: _____

Where to Dine?
List a few spots you're considering for this letter-choices make it fun!:

The Winner Is...
Write your pick and note what made it stand out:

Savor the Moment!
Share a quick highlight of your experience-the dishes, vibe, and details:

Rating: ☆☆☆☆☆

Memory Lane...
Snap a photo that captures the moment, be sure to get the name in the shot, so you'll always remember this stop of your journey!

Who Shared This Meal?
Whether you were solo, with friends, or family, describe who joined you!

Date: _____

Where to Dine?
List a few spots you're considering for this letter-choices make it fun!:

The Winner Is...
Write your pick and note what made it stand out:

Savor the Moment!
Share a quick highlight of your experience-the dishes, vibe, and details:

Rating: ☆☆☆☆☆

Memory Lane...
Snap a photo that captures the moment, be sure to get the name in the shot, so you'll always remember this stop of your journey!

Who Shared This Meal?
Whether you were solo, with friends, or family, describe who joined you!

Date: _____

'Z

Where to Dine?
List a few spots you're considering for this letter-choices make it fun!:

The Winner Is...
Write your pick and note what made it stand out:

Savor the Moment!
Share a quick highlight of your experience-the dishes, vibe, and details:

Rating: ☆☆☆☆☆

Z

Memory Lane...
Snap a photo that captures the moment, be sure to get the name in the shot, so you'll always remember this stop of your journey!

Who Shared This Meal?
Whether you were solo, with friends, or family, describe who joined you!

Made in the USA
Columbia, SC
19 February 2025

54107169R00030